I0902025

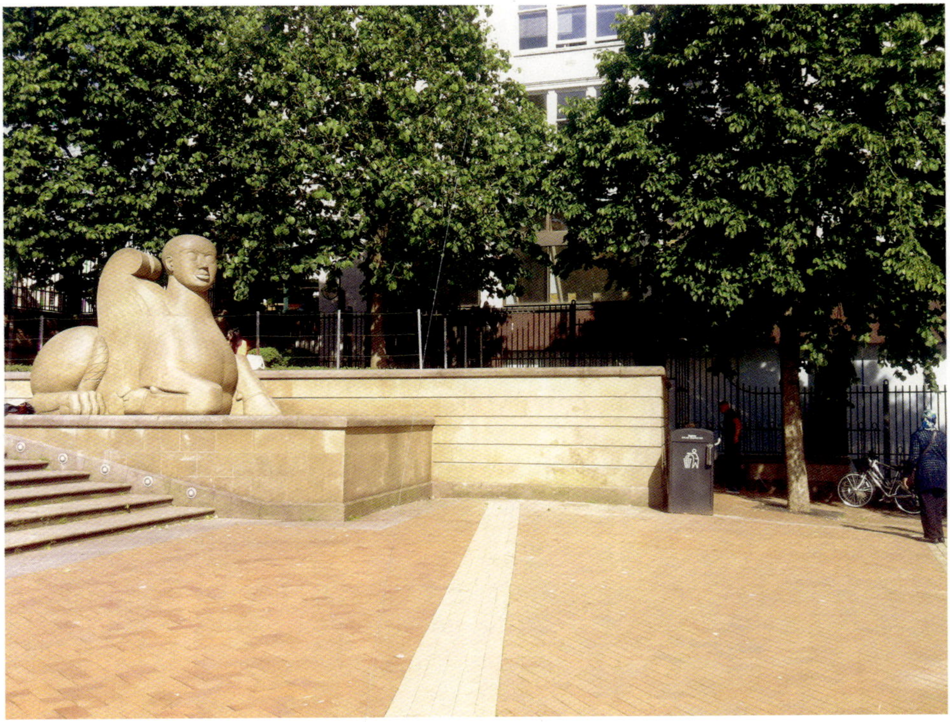

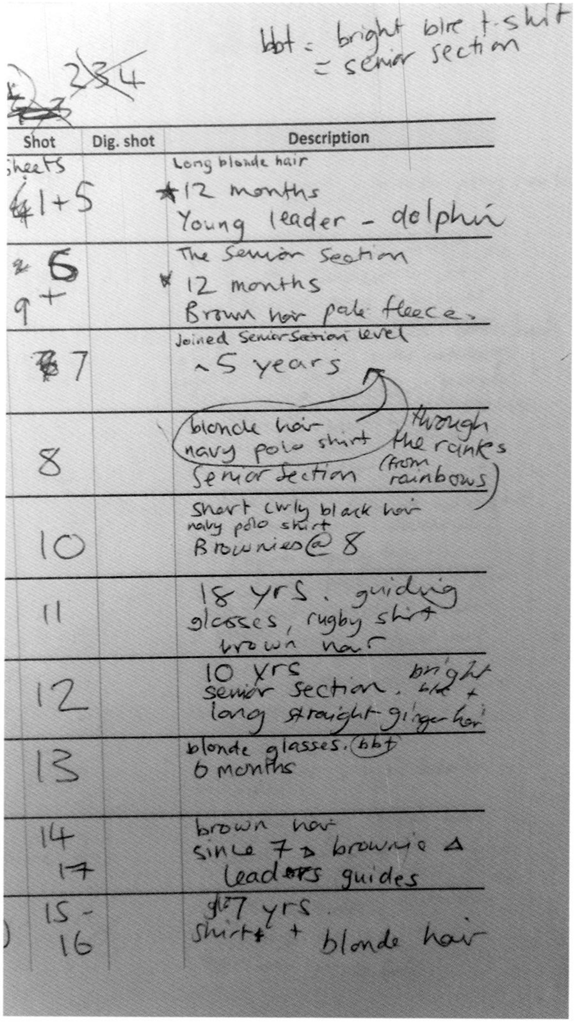

bbt = bright blue t-shirt
= senior section

2 3 4

Shot	Dig. shot	Description
sheets 1+5		Long blonde hair ★12 months Young leader – dolphin
6 9+		The Senior Section ★ 12 months Brown hair pale fleece.
7		Joined Senior Section level ~5 years
8		blonde hair navy polo shirt Senior Section through the ranks (from rainbows)
10		short curly black hair navy polo shirt Brownies @ 8
11		18 yrs. guiding glasses, rugby shirt brown hair
12		10 yrs senior section. bright blue t long straight ginger hair
13		blonde glasses. (bbt) 6 months
14 17		brown hair since 7 → brownie → leaders guides
15 – 16		7 yrs. shirt + blonde hair

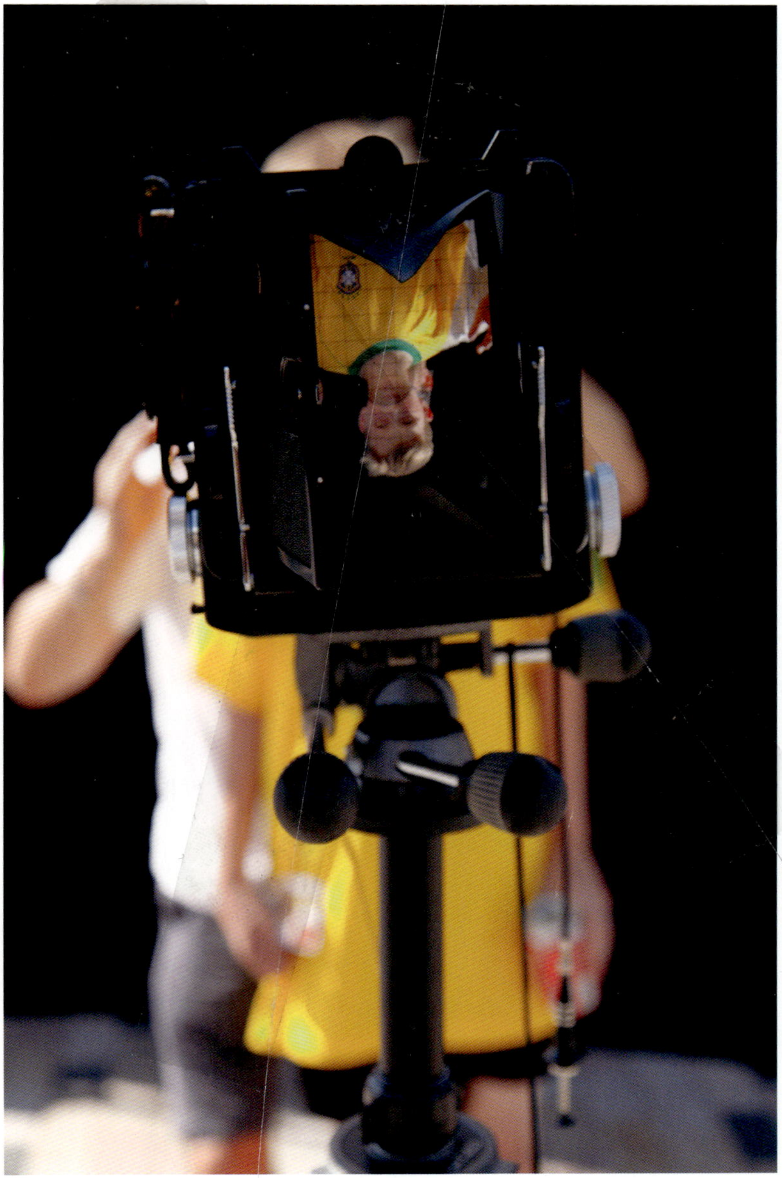

Trevor: Are you an only child?

Sarah: Yeah, I am an only child, which comes with its pros and cons I guess.

Trevor: Yeah?

Sarah: Yeah.

Trevor: Did you want to talk about that?

Sarah: It doesn't really bother me.

Trevor: I've got a child, I've got one child and he's an only child and I worry about that...

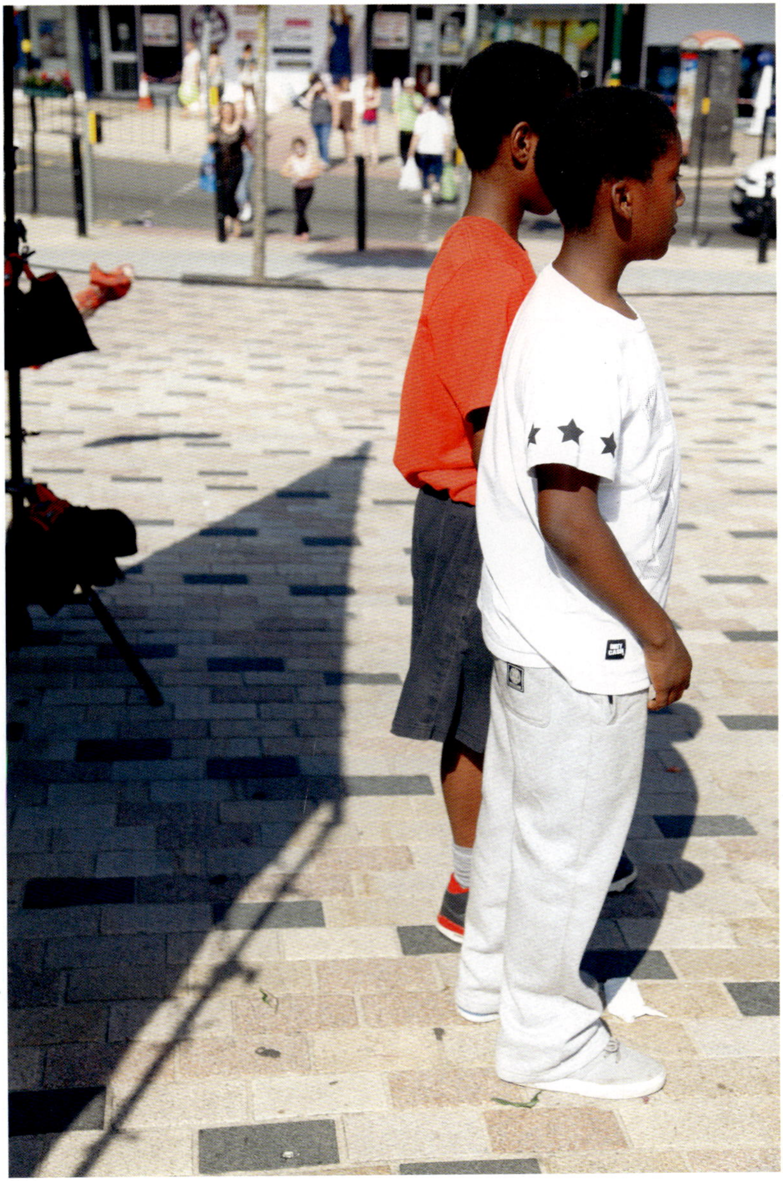

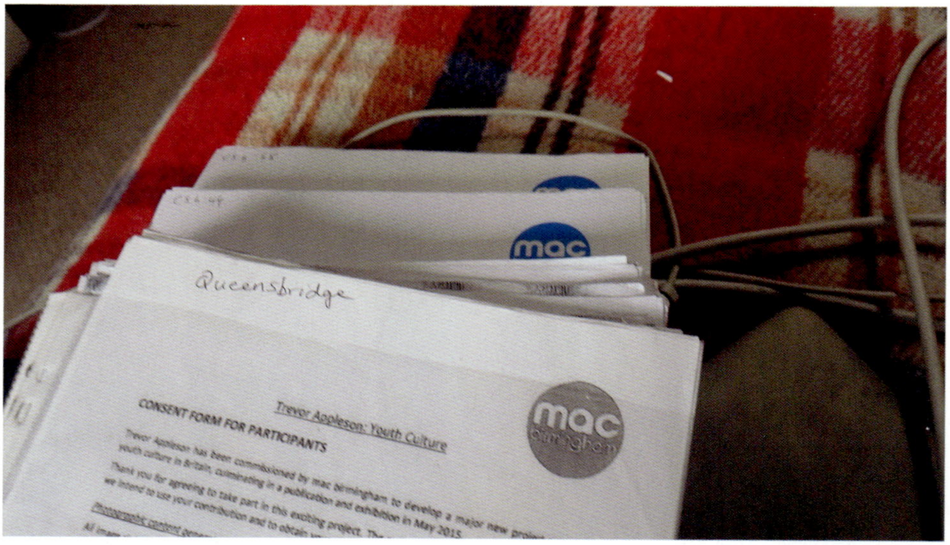
mac
mac
Queensbridge
Trevor Appleson: Youth Culture
CONSENT FORM FOR PARTICIPANTS
mac
birmingham

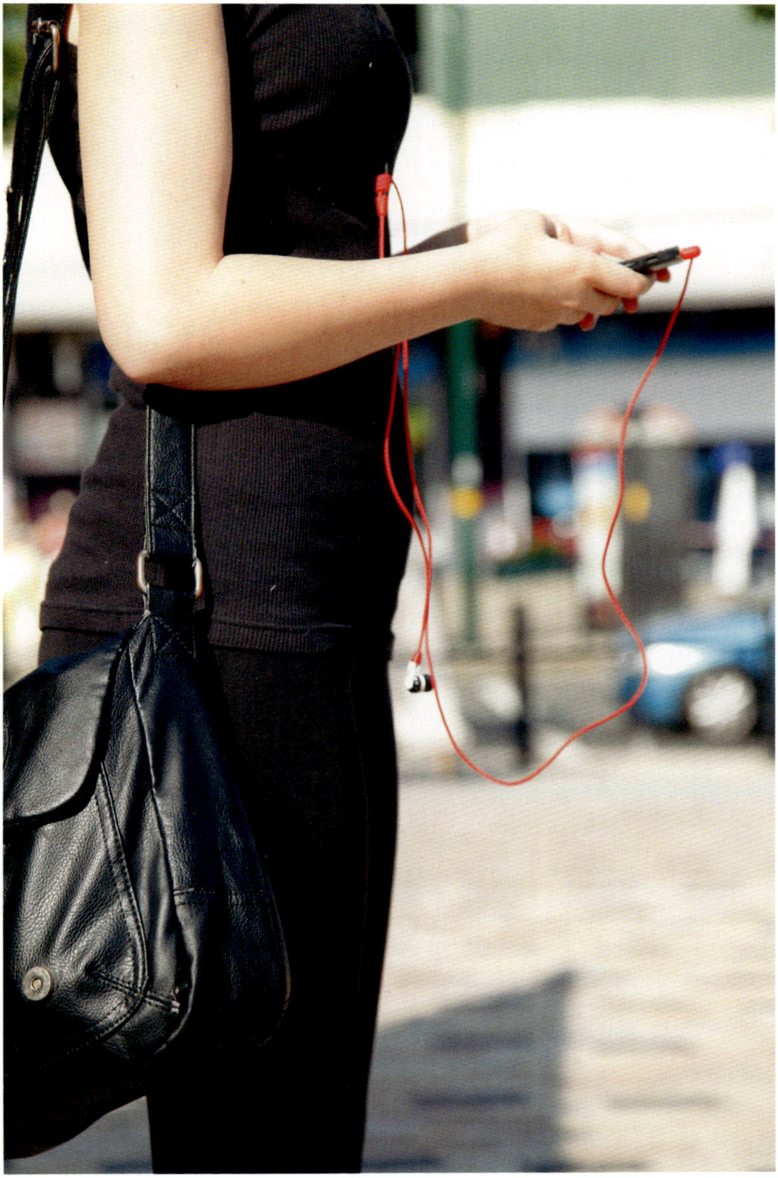

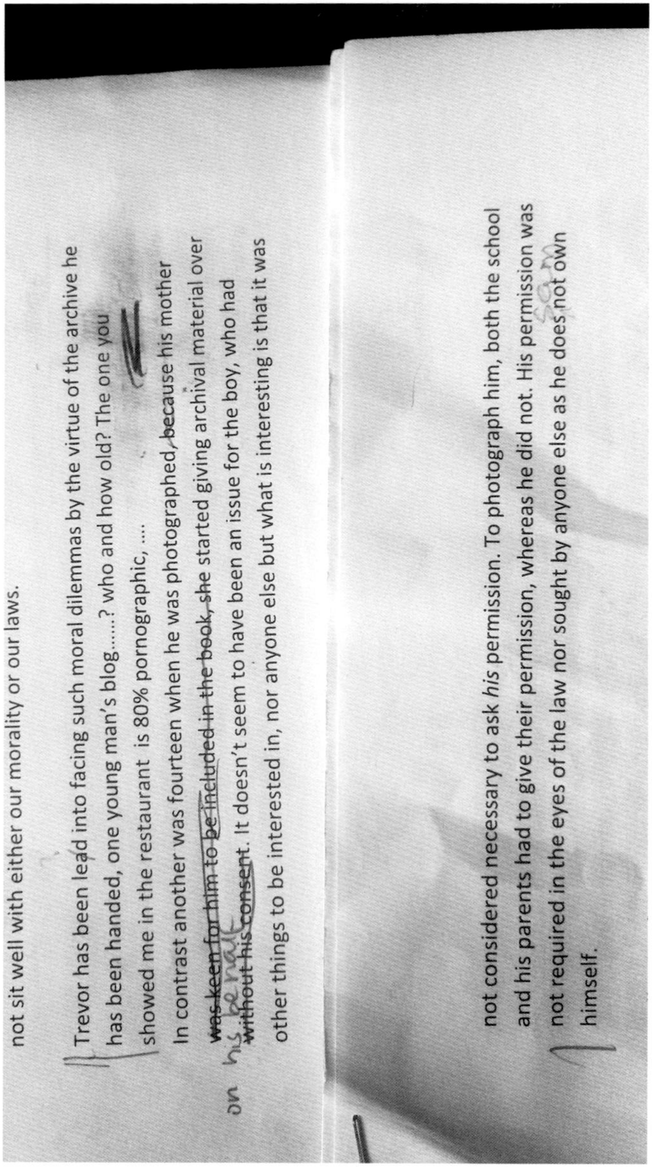

not sit well with either our morality or our laws.

Trevor has been lead into facing such moral dilemmas by the virtue of the archive he has been handed, one young man's blog......? who and how old? The one you showed me in the restaurant is 80% pornographic, ...
In contrast another was fourteen when he was photographed, ~~because his mother was keen for him to be included in the book, she~~ started giving archival material over ~~without his consent~~. It doesn't seem to have been an issue for the boy, who had other things to be interested in, nor anyone else but what is interesting is that it was

not considered necessary to ask *his* permission. To photograph him, both the school and his parents had to give their permission, whereas he did not. His permission was not required in the eyes of the law nor sought by anyone else as he does not own himself.

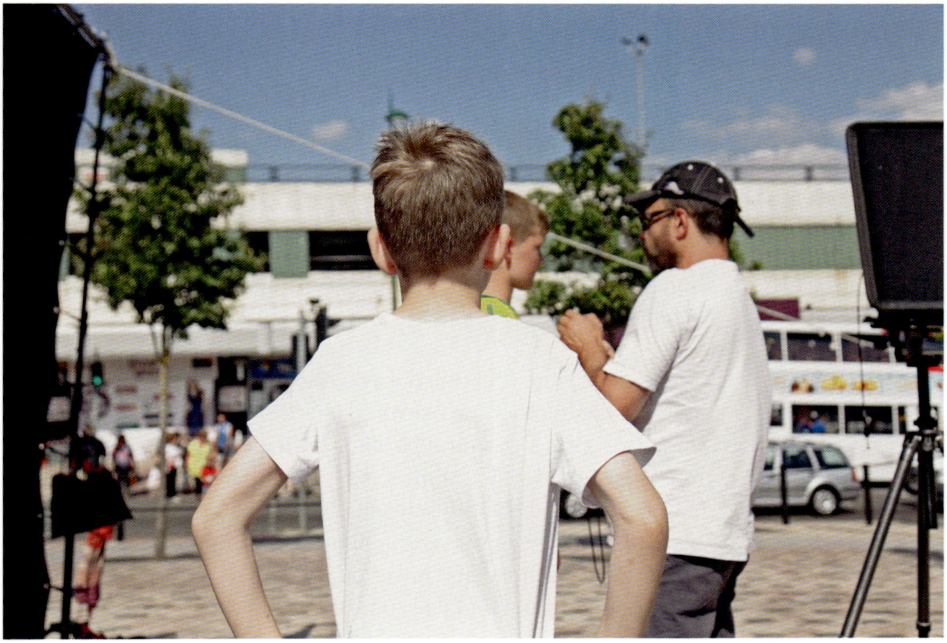

Trevor: So – you said you were pissed by the time you arrived at work, so you had a beer for breakfast?

Francis: Yeah, you could say that.

Trevor: Yeah?

Francis: But that's because I was still hung over from last night. (Laughter)

Trevor: From last night?

Francis: Yeah.

Trevor: Okay. So, you had a gig last night, so you basically just continued?

Francis: Yeah, yeah. Basically.

Trevor: Fran, can you get me some pictures of your family? Some pictures of your parents and your grandparents?

Francis: Erm … well … no. Put it this way – like my granddad and my grandmother were divorced in the 80s. They were alive when I was born but they both died by the time I was two. See … I think there's one of my nan and my granddad actually, my mum's parents. I've seen that. But I've never seen a photo of my granddad – my Greek granddad and my gran. I've seen – there's pictures of my mum and dad somewhere but they're like photos of me and … them like when I was a baby. Yeah. But my mum is a bit like protective of them photos, to be honest. Because they mean a lot to her, you know? She won't let me have them. She won't let anybody have them. I remember like before Becky came round to my mum's house.

Trevor: Yeah.

Francis: She said – "They're my photos, they're my photos."

Trevor: Okay. Alright.

Francis: You can use any of the photos that are on Facebook.

Trevor: Okay, yeah, I know. I know, for me, what I'm also interested in is unpacking histories.

Francis: Oh, yeah.

Trevor: Not just kind of now, because when you look at people's histories it's very powerful. It's ...

Francis: I understand mate.

Francis: Yeah, there must be a photo of my granddad and my grandma somewhere, but I've never seen – I've only ever seen one photo of my granddad when he was young and he looked like the Greek Elvis.

Trevor: Those kind of pictures are priceless.

Trevor: So, what does kind of like youth culture mean to you? Because I think...what is youth culture really? I was commissioned by a museum here – that's how this whole project started – to look at youth culture in the city, and I think that's a very hard thing actually...

Francis: I think you'd better go and ask somebody ten years younger than me, you know what I'm saying? You're asking someone who's 25 about youth culture. I'm a fully-grown man now, you know what I'm saying?

Trevor: When I was 25, I still almost felt like a boy, or has society changed? – because when I was ... when I was a teenager in South Africa, there was no internet. And there were no mobile phones. They only came when I was 24, 25. At your age is when the mobile phone arrived.

Francis: No way, man.

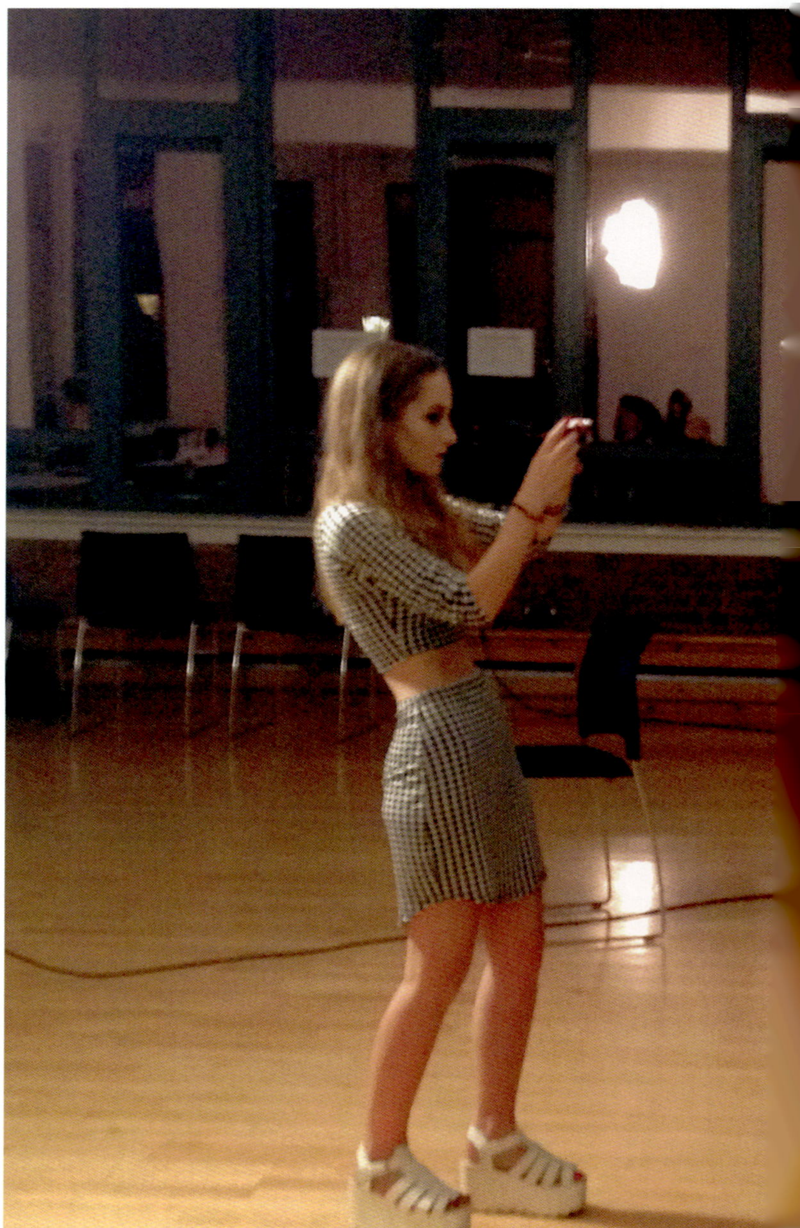

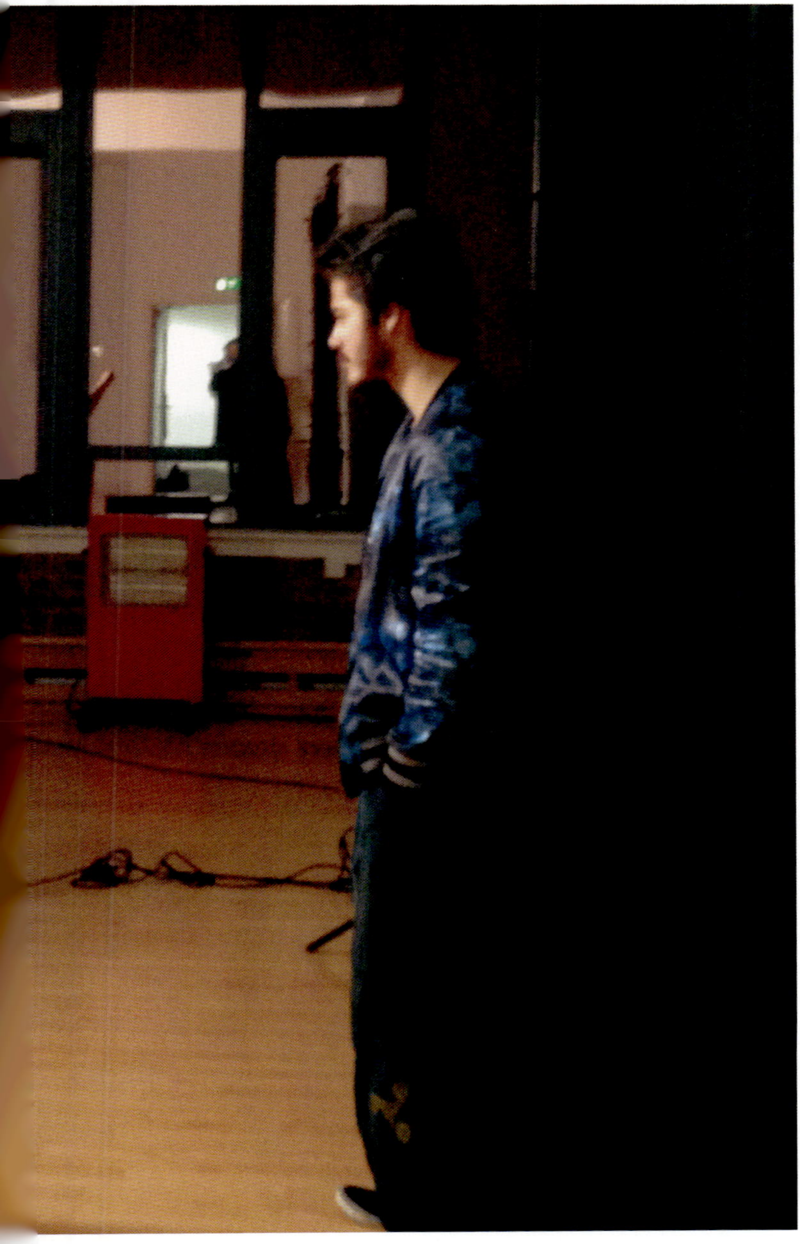

Trevor: I was one of the first of my friends to get a mobile phone. (Laughter)

Trevor: And it was like, "What is this?" We all had 'pagers' before that.

Francis: Yeah. Pagers.
(Laughter)

Francis: Yeah, it's like text messages before there was phones (Laughter)

Trevor: What do you understand – what does the word "youth culture" mean to you?

Francis: The culture of a youth, but the problem is with that, is that youths are indecisive. They don't know what they like yet because they haven't really experienced much. Like, I remember one geezer when I was younger, like he'd be a Goth one week, then he'd be like a Chav, then he'd be an Emo, then a Skater then … It's like he'd just be everything, so you can't really say "youth culture" because that's what I'm saying, they haven't found their culture yet. Is what I'd say.

Trevor: Yeah, I mean … my point is, that, I'm mostly left wondering if there is such a thing as 'youth culture'…

Francis: I believe that too. Only because they're too undecided.

Trevor: But you know, I've done this project, and we've done shoots around the city at different locations, like a Saturday night on Broad Street, and we did a rave, and outside your punk gig, we shot in Centenary Square a couple of times, and Victoria Square and –

Francis: See, that would be a good place to find out about youth culture. When they have the hipster meetings, all them ones with the multi-coloured hair and all that.

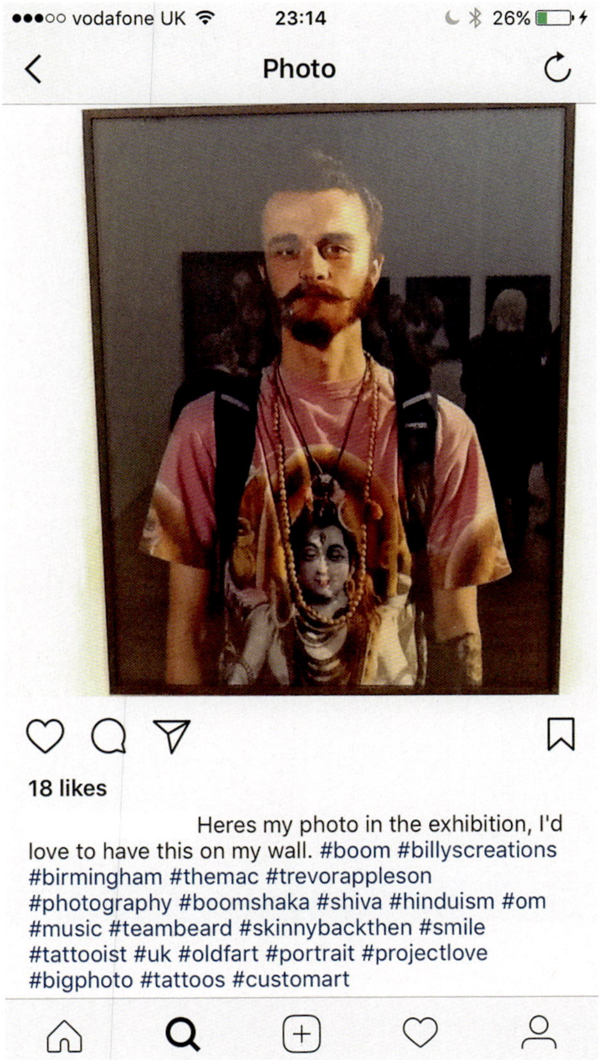
vodafone UK
23:14
26%
Photo
18 likes
Heres my photo in the exhibition, I'd love to have this on my wall. #boom #billyscreations #birmingham #themac #trevorappleson #photography #boomshaka #shiva #hinduism #om #music #teambeard #skinnybackthen #smile #tattooist #uk #oldfart #portrait #projectlove #bigphoto #tattoos #customart

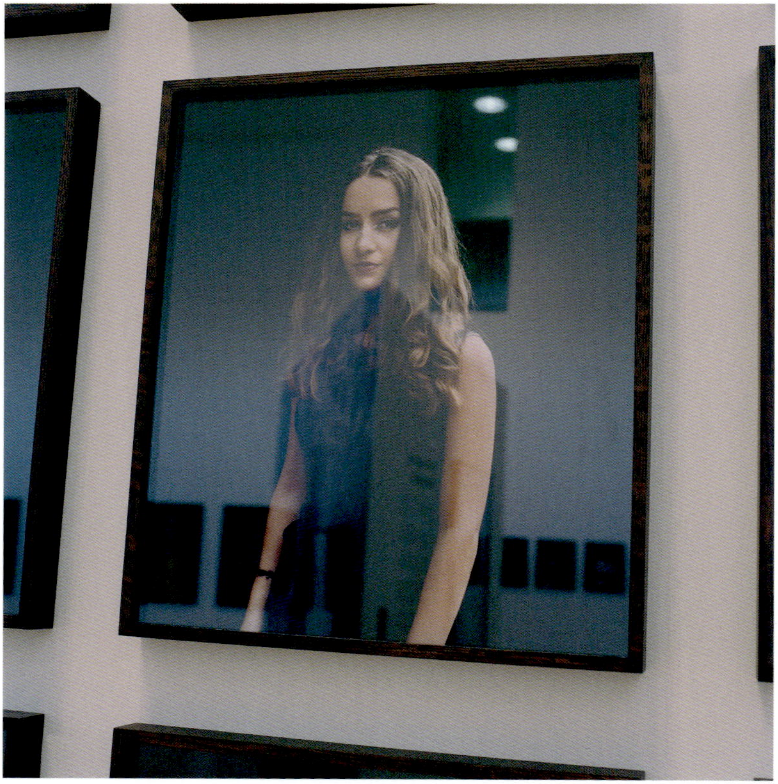

…York Pop and the 'cool' style of photography.

The circle has now been fully described: fractions of youth now aspire to the flatness and the stillness of a photograph. They are completed only through the admiring glances of a stranger.

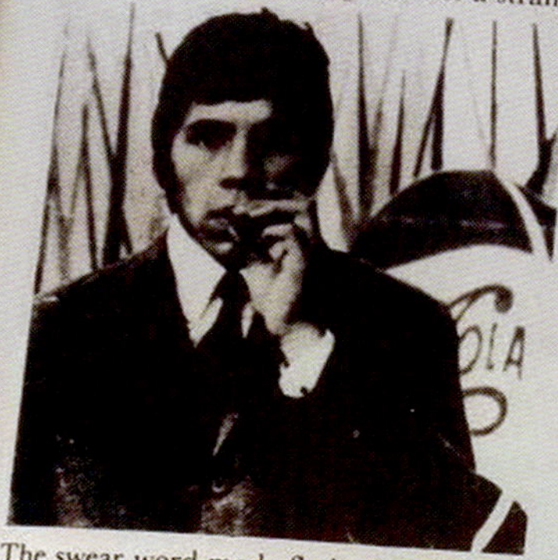

The swear word made flesh: 'youth culture' as sign-system centres on the body – on appearance, posture, dress. If teenagers possess little else, they at least own their own bodies. If power can be exercised nowhere else, it can at least be exercised here.

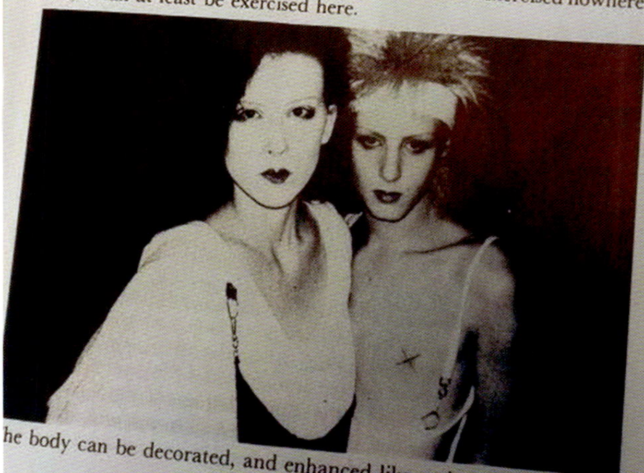

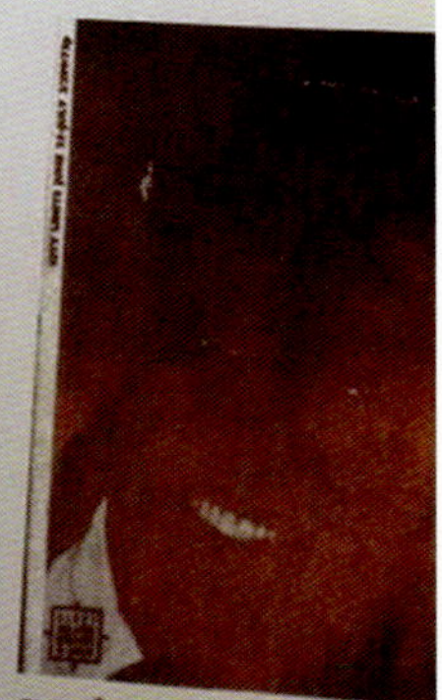

youth as fun

[T]he body can be decorated, and enhanced like a cherished object.

31

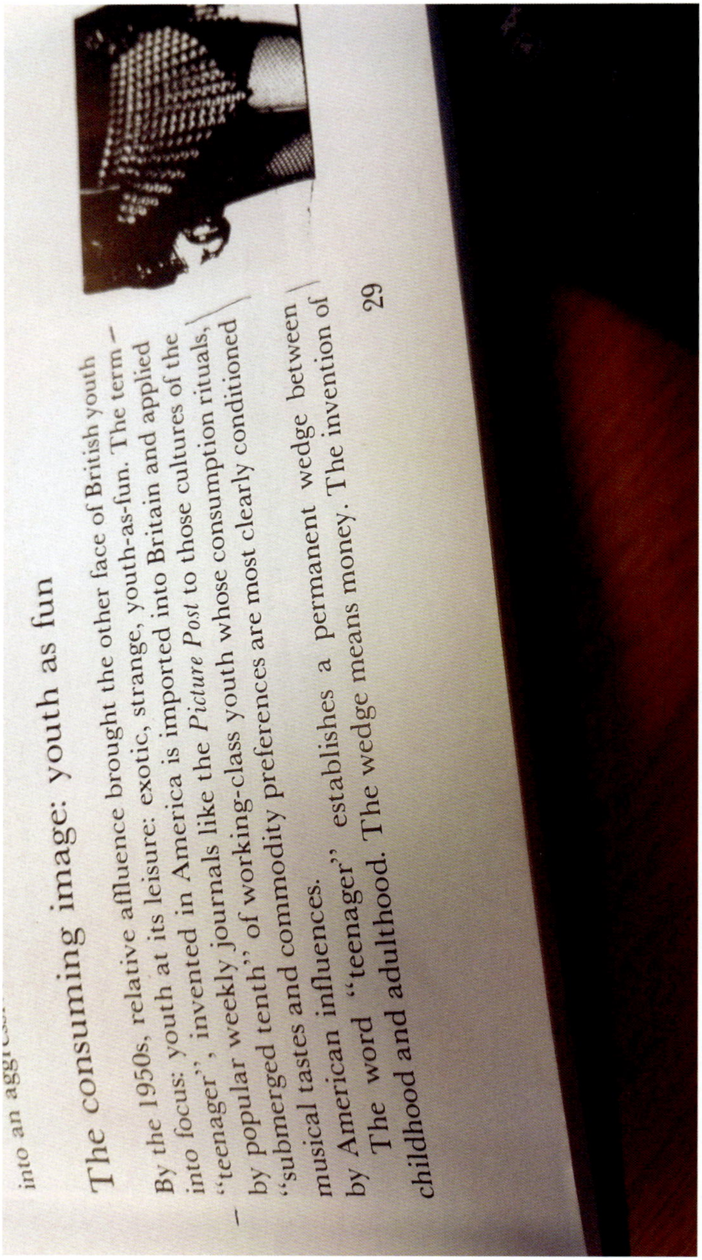

into an aggres

The consuming image: youth as fun

By the 1950s, relative affluence brought the other face of British youth into focus: youth at its leisure: exotic, strange, youth-as-fun. The term – "teenager", invented in America is imported into Britain and applied by popular weekly journals like the *Picture Post* to those cultures of the "submerged tenth" of working-class youth whose consumption rituals, musical tastes and commodity preferences are most clearly conditioned by American influences.

The word "teenager" establishes a permanent wedge between childhood and adulthood. The wedge means money. The invention of

29

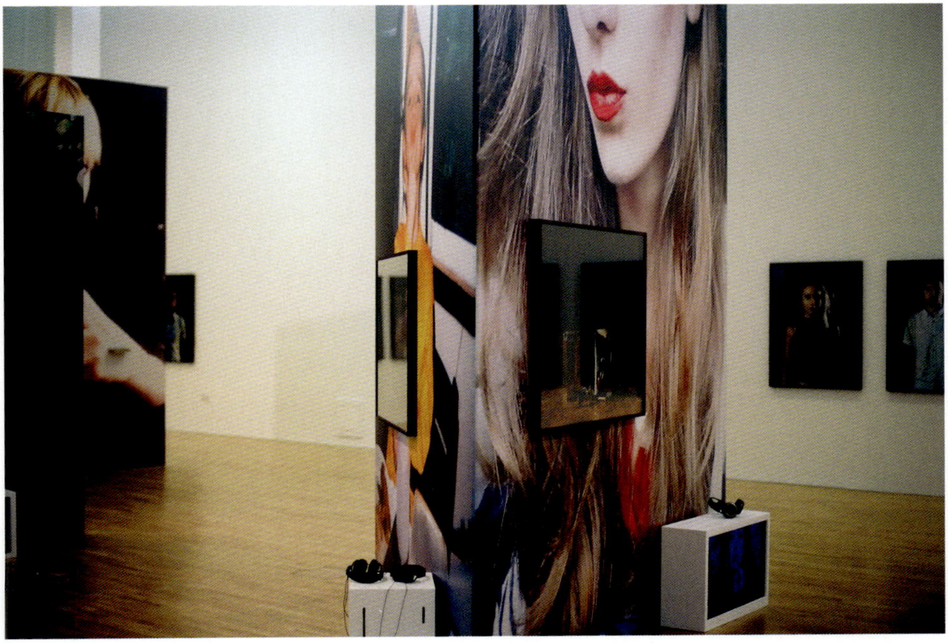

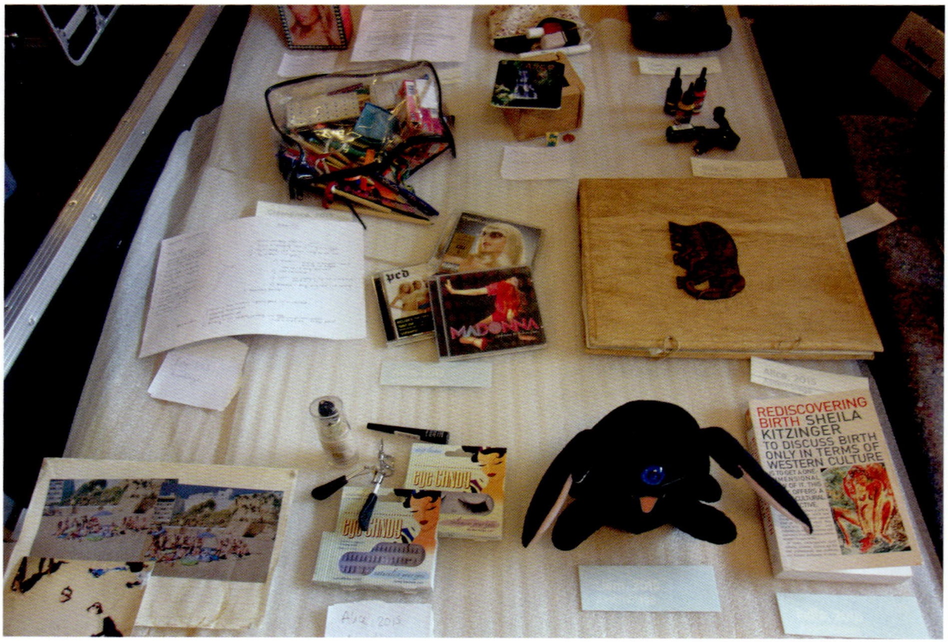
REDISCOVERING BIRTH SHEILA KITZINGER
TO DISCUSS BIRTH ONLY IN TERMS OF WESTERN CULTURE
MADONNA

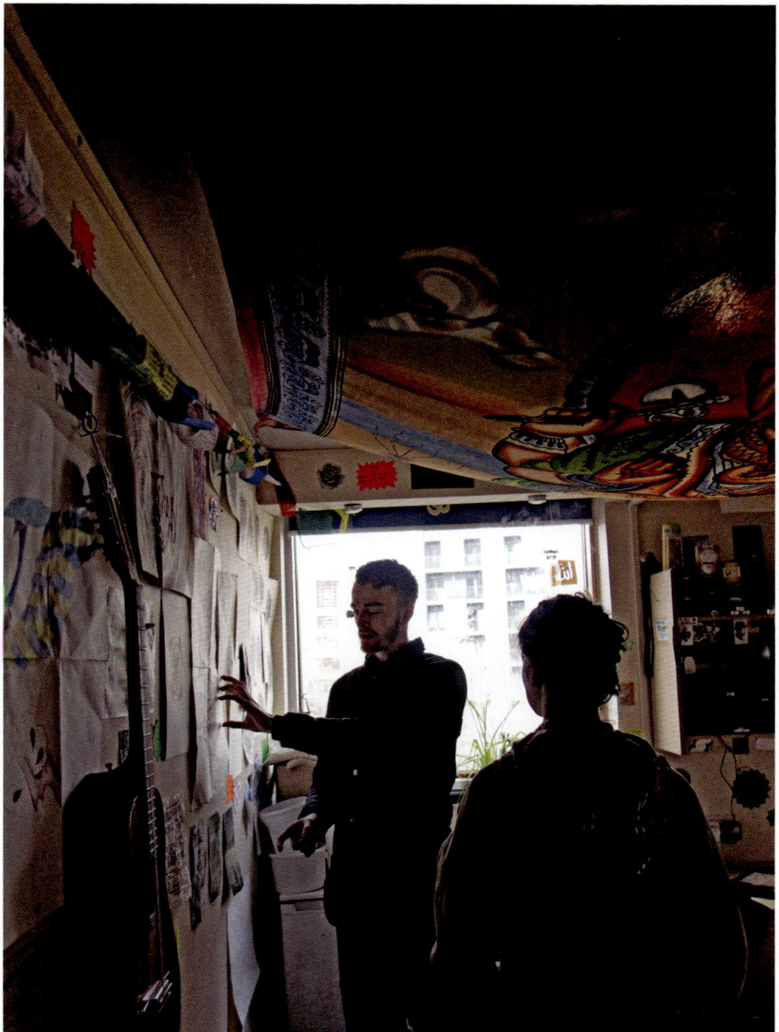

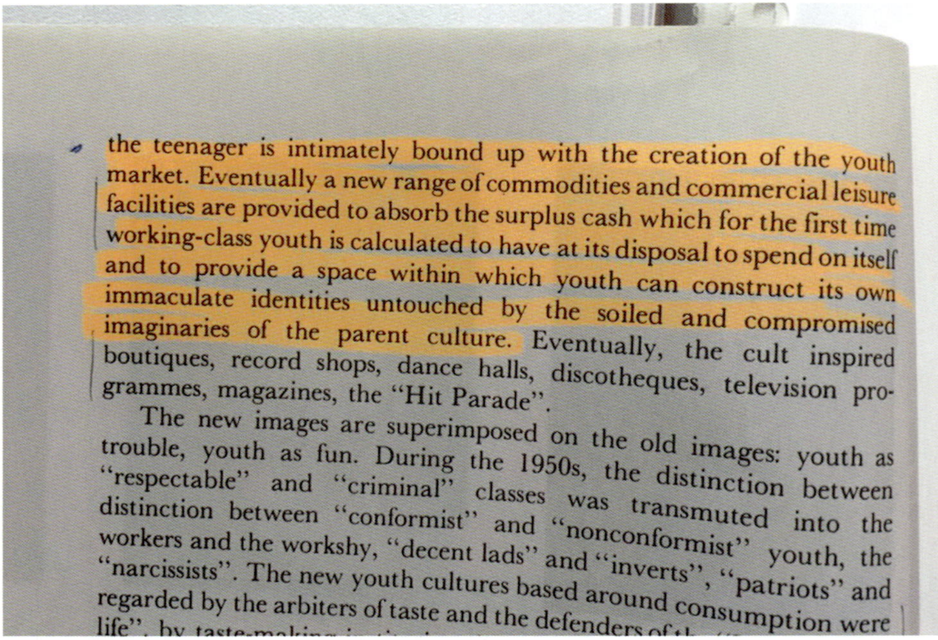

the teenager is intimately bound up with the creation of the youth market. Eventually a new range of commodities and commercial leisure facilities are provided to absorb the surplus cash which for the first time working-class youth is calculated to have at its disposal to spend on itself and to provide a space within which youth can construct its own immaculate identities untouched by the soiled and compromised imaginaries of the parent culture. Eventually, the cult inspired boutiques, record shops, dance halls, discotheques, television programmes, magazines, the "Hit Parade".

The new images are superimposed on the old images: youth as trouble, youth as fun. During the 1950s, the distinction between "respectable" and "criminal" classes was transmuted into the distinction between "conformist" and "nonconformist" youth, the workers and the workshy, "decent lads" and "inverts", "patriots" and "narcissists". The new youth cultures based around consumption were regarded by the arbiters of taste and the defenders of the ...

life", by

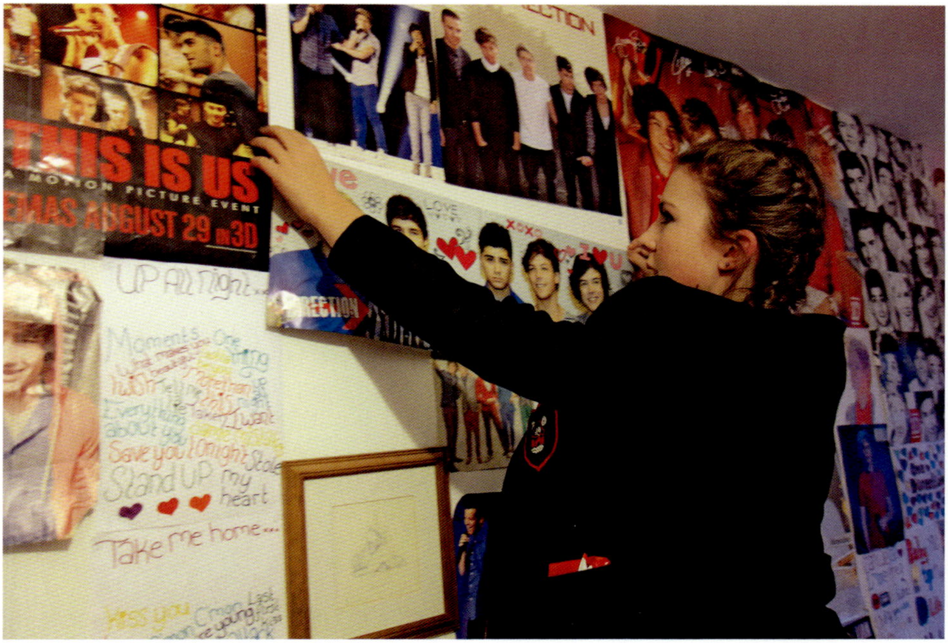
THIS IS US
A MOTION PICTURE EVENT
Up All Night...
Save you tonight
Stand Up
Take me home...

8. The various archival collections placed in a depositary must be kept carefully separate.

16. The system of arrangement must be based on the original organisation of the archival collection, which in the main corresponds to the organisation of the administrative body that produced it.

19. In the arrangement of an archival collection the interests of historical research should receive only secondary consideration

21. It is not the subject of a document but its destination, which must determine the place it is to occupy in the archival collection.

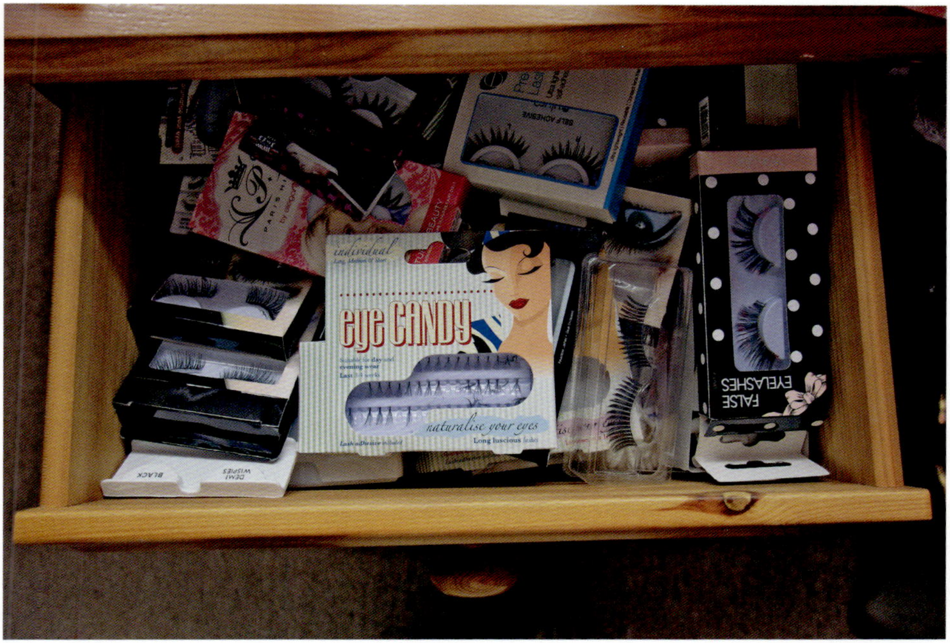
individual
eye CANDY
naturalise your eyes
FALSE EYELASHES
SELF ADHESIVE
DEMI WISPIES
BLACK

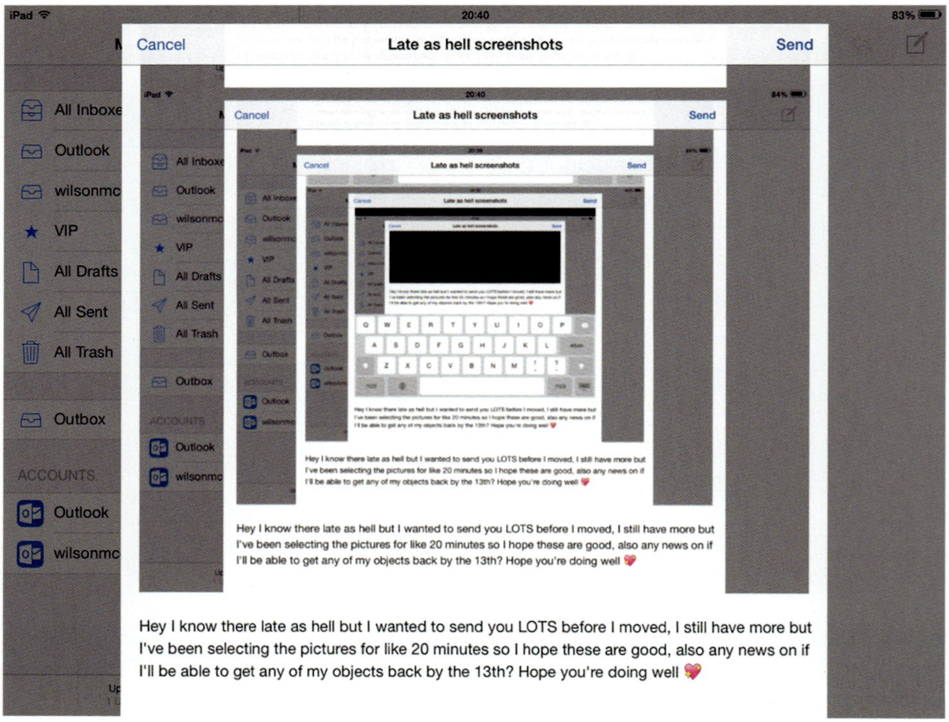
iPad
20:40
83%
Cancel
Late as hell screenshots
Send
All Inboxe
Outlook
wilsonmc
VIP
All Drafts
All Sent
All Trash
Outbox
ACCOUNTS
Outlook
wilsonmc
Hey I know there late as hell but I wanted to send you LOTS before I moved, I still have more but I've been selecting the pictures for like 20 minutes so I hope these are good, also any news on if I'll be able to get any of my objects back by the 13th? Hope you're doing well 💖

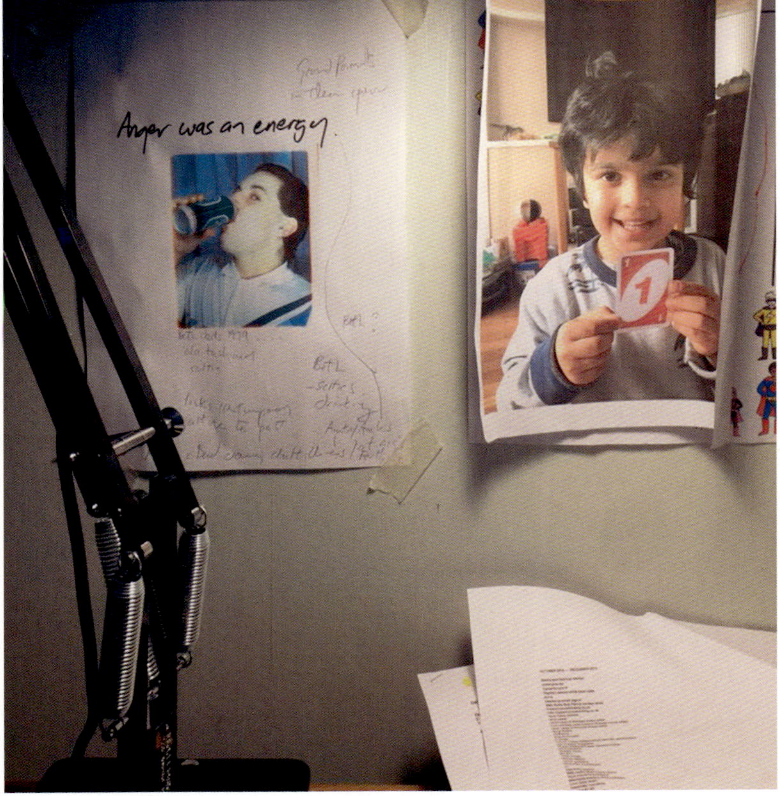
Anger was an energy.

Appendix

Front cover: Nicole. (Appleson, T. (2017) *Portable Studio*. London: Booth-Clibborn Editions, p.69, 414–433)

1, 5, 7, 9.
Northfield High Street, Birmingham, 24 July 2014. (*Portable Studio*, p.54–63) Photographs, Ayesha Jones.

2. Interview excerpt: Trevor and Sarah, 6 June 2016. (*Portable Studio*, p.99, 708–733)

3. Location shot: Victoria Square, Birmingham, 7 July 2014. (*Portable Studio*, p.11–34)

4. Shoot documentation: Guides. (*Portable Studio*, p.46–53)

6. Consent forms: Queensbridge School. (*Portable Studio*, p.5–10)

8. Gore, J. (2016) 'I love you guys', unpublished essay.

10, 11, 14.
Interview excerpts: Trevor and Francis, 6 June 2016. (*Portable Studio*, p.101, 738–755)

12, 13.
Alice's party, mac birmingham, 6 December 2016. (*Portable Studio*, p.35–45) Photograph, Becky Sexton.

15. Screenshot of Billy's social media post, June 2015. (*Portable Studio*, p.93, 632–653)

16, 19.
Trevor Appleson, *Birmingham*, mac birmingham (2 May–5 July 2015), photographed 5 July 2015.

17, 18, 22.
Hebdige, D. (1998) *Hiding in the light*, London: Routledge.

20. Selected objects in mac birmingham storeroom, June 2016.

21. Home visit: Billy, 18 February 2014. (*Portable Studio*, p.93, 632–653) Photograph, Becky Sexton.

23. Home visit: Eden, 15 December 2014. Photograph, Becky Sexton.

24. Muller, Fz S., Feith, J.A. and Fruin R. Leavitt A.H (translator) (1940) *Manual for the Arrangement and Description of Archives*. New York: The H Wilson Company.
26. Wilson's screenshot, 9 September 2015. (*Portable Studio*, p.37, 312–339)
27. The artist's studio: photographs of Beth's dad (*Portable Studio*, p.102, 728–733) and artist's child (2017).

Back cover: Email communication between co-editor, artist and participants.

Hi ~~India,~~

Good to hear from you. Trevor is photographing the archive now, so we should be able to return your items in the next couple of months.

Thanks again for your patience, and apologies for the unforeseen delay. It is proving to be an enormous project but we're very excited about the final product, hope you are too.

Hope all is well with you.

best wishes
~~Chloe~~

Dear ~~Chloe,~~

Sounds fantastic, I'm very eager to see the final outcome. It sounds amazing from when I've spoken with Trevor.

It would be good if I could get at least some of my things back before Christmas as I've given a lot of sentimental objects, so would like to have them back safe at home soon. Would this be possible?

Thanks so much
~~India~~

Hi ~~India,~~

Thanks for your messages. Should be fine to get these back to you by Christmas. Please bear with us, as really is a mammoth task we have undertaken here! All is being stored safely, so please do not worry.

In regards to the interview we were speaking about. We are working with a writer, Dr Joanna Gore, who would like to talk to you/interview you for a text piece she's writing. Would this be OK? She would like to focus on your instagram and your tablet box you gave.

Please let me know, and we will set up the interview as soon as.

All the best
~~Trevor~~

Dear ~~Chloe,~~
Could you please update me on the wheareabouts of my personal belongings as I have not heard from you for a while and am still out of the country so will need to inform someone in Birmingham to help me get them back
Thanks

Hi ~~Louise,~~

Your personal objects are still in Trevor's studio. I will pass your message on and he will be in touch as soon as he in a position to return them.

Thanks again for your patience. Hope you are having a good time abroad.

Best wishes
~~Chloe~~

ISBN 978-1-86154-380-6